ate Due

MAKING MEN WHOLE

By J. B. Phillips

LETTERS TO YOUNG CHURCHES
  A translation of the New Testament Epistles
THE GOSPELS *translated into Modern English*
YOUR GOD IS TOO SMALL
MAKING MEN WHOLE

J. B. PHILLIPS

Making Men Whole

New York
THE MACMILLAN COMPANY
1956

CONTENTS

CONTENTS

FOREWORD

THE FOLLOWING FIVE CHAPTERS REPRESENT THE SUBSTANCE OF THE
Bible Readings which I was asked to give during the first week
of the Church Missionary Society Summer School at Bangor in
1952. The title, *Making Men Whole,* represents the dominant
thought of our prayer and study together. As an introduction to
the appearance of these Bible Readings in book form, I would
underline the following points which seem to me basic to our
theme:

1. Many Christians suffer to-day, more perhaps than in any
preceding age, from a sense that the world is out of control. The
impact of world tensions and problems is often so great that
Christians, because they see and feel and care more than non-
Christians, frequently become over-anxious and exaggerate their
own responsibilities. We all need to be reminded that God is by
no means baffled or bewildered by mankind's muddles and follies.
We all need to remember that our strength lies in quietness and
confidence, not in frantic challenges and hysterical efforts. The
world remains primarily God's responsibility, and the best we
can do is to find out our own part in His vast purpose and make
sure that we are fulfilling that to the limit of our ability.

2. Most Christians are affected far more than they know by
the standards and methods of the surrounding world. In these
days when power and size and speed are almost universally ad-
mired, it seems to me particularly important to study afresh the
"weakness," the "smallness of entry" and the "slowness" of God
as He began His vast work of reconstructing His disordered world.

7

We are all tempted to take short cuts, to work for quick results and to evade painful sacrifice. It is therefore essential that we should look again at love incarnate in a human being, to see God Himself at work within the limitations of human personality, and to base our methods on what we see Him do.

3. The writers of the New Testament Epistles never regarded the Christian religion as an "ethic," still less a performance. To them it was an invasion of their own lives by the living Spirit of God; their response in repentance and faith provided the means by which the divine could penetrate the merely human. They lived lives of super-human quality because they believed quite simply that Christ Himself was alive within them.

For some reason or other we seem to regard this belief as somewhat presumptuous, and much of our present-day Christianity is a rather gauche performance designed to please an external God. The real presumption, indeed the impertinence, of our modern attitude is that we do not really accept God's full generosity; we do not really believe that Christ is alive and operative in every true disciple.

4. The pressure of world events, as well as of the gentle leading of the Spirit of God Himself, is making it plain to the dimmest human intelligence that men must learn to live together as one family or perish from the earth altogether. Thus I believe that we can say, without unduly dramatizing ourselves, that we live in a time of great acceleration of God's "one increasing purpose." In Christ alone is there integration for the individual, for the Churches, and for the whole scattered human family. The purpose itself, in its scope and depth, is becoming clearer, and the most important issue confronting any one of us is the question: "Am *I* co-operating with the purpose, or not?"

5. If we are to have a "whole" view of life and its purpose, it is very necessary for us to recover the sense that this human life of ours is lived *sub specie aeternitatis*. In our modern preoccupation with Christian social justice and the relevance of the Christian faith to all human problems, we tend to forget the heaven to

which we are bound. Unless we have this essential background, we are left with too many unsolved problems and too many flagrant injustices for us to believe confidently in the love of God. Quite apart from the question of rewards, punishments and compensations, we do not allow God sufficient "elbow-room" in this restricted sphere for the final working out of His awful patient purpose. We must recover the wonder and glory of the calling wherewith we are called.

Nothing that I have written is new; all of it is based on the Scripture passages which are at the head of each chapter. But we need constantly to be reminded of those eternal truths by which alone we can face this life with courage, hope and good humour.

J. B. PHILLIPS

ST. JOHN'S VICARAGE
REDHILL, SURREY

I

GOD AND
A WORLD DISINTEGRATED

Passages which should be studied in connexion with the following chapter are:

ST. JOHN X. verses 1 to 16
EPHESIANS ii. verses 4 to 18

I

GOD AND

A WORLD DISINTEGRATED

WE FACE TO-DAY A WORLD TORN AND DIVIDED. SO WIDESPREAD IS THE distress of nations, so complex the problems which face every thinking Christian, that I think we may be forgiven if our hearts sometimes fail us. There is no need to elaborate here the problems and distresses which confront us on every hand. Probably we are only too well aware of them. But for our comfort we may fairly remind ourselves that the world-wide tensions and sufferings only seem to us to be more overwhelming than they did to our forefathers because we are much better informed about them through modern means of news-transmission than they could ever be. To-day, with vastly improved communications of all kinds, we are aware of what is happening in distant places, whereas our forefathers could live much more parochially and usually with little sense of world problems.

This difference is not, of course, entirely a matter of news communication, for during the last century the nations have become infinitely more inter-dependent than ever before in the history of the world. To be isolationist or parochial has become not only un-Christian but impossible. What happens in China, or Africa or the United States can no longer be of merely academic interest to us; it can affect profoundly our actual lives. A

hundred years ago or less, it would have been fantastic to suggest that a struggle in far-off Korea, for example, could have the
faintest bearing on the private life of an ordinary Englishman,
even if he knew about it. To-day we are so inter-related that the
problems of distant countries affect not merely our minds and
hearts but our very mode of living, whether we like it or not. In
days gone by there could be famines, plagues, bitter wars, earth-
quakes and disasters, happening perhaps on a vast scale in a far-
away continent, and we should have known nothing of them. But
to-day we hear of these things, we read of them, we see pictures of
them on the news-reels, and even the least sensitive can hardly say,
"This is no concern of mine."

To put it another way, the vast achievements of science through
improved travelling, and communications have borne in upon
the sensitive soul, and more slowly upon the insensitive, the fact
that we are, however divided, "all in it together." There has
never been a time in the history of the world when men have
thought and calculated in global terms as to-day they must. And
there is, of course, no arresting of this progress, no preventing of
the awakening from sleep of continent and race. We as Christians
are probably more sensitive than anyone else to the fact that for
the first time in the history of the human race men have got to
learn to live together as a family. And because we know how
deep-rooted are human sins and frailties, we are more aware
than others of how difficult this problem must inevitably be.

We need not, however, be overwhelmed by the prospect before
us, for two reasons. First, because this is God's world, and although we may be bewildered by the speed at which the world
is awakening before our eyes, we can be quite sure that there is
no bewilderment in the mind of God. This is His world; and
since He knows the end from the beginning we can at all times be
confident that at any given moment in the world's history there
is, for those who will listen to His voice, a right way of meeting
the complexities of the contemporary situation, even though that

right way cannot in the nature of things achieve in a single generation the perfect will of God.

Then again, we need constantly to remind ourselves that no single one of us and no single group of us is required to carry more responsibility than we can bear. We may well feel battered, bruised and bewildered by the continual assault of news, of problems put before us, of challenges thrown down to us. But each man has his proper work to do, and no single one of us is required to do more than the will of God for him. The famous words, "In His will is our peace," are perfectly true here as in other contexts. If we attempt to do more than His will, if we allow ourselves to be stampeded into responsibilities beyond our powers by the vastness of the problems around us, we lose our peace. We need, as St. Paul told the Thessalonians, "to study to be quiet and to do our business" (1 Thessalonians iv. 11). In doing our part of God's will we shall find peace, but in attempting more than our part we shall find only anxiety and frustration.

This truth needs to be thought out by all who share a common interest in the world-wide work of the Church. We can so easily become tense and over-anxious just because we are sensitive to the world's need, and thereby fail effectually to do that small part of the task which God has allotted to us. Because of the magnitude of the problems which press upon us, we may even seek to evade such frightening responsibilities. But if we will keep in mind the fact that the ultimate responsibility belongs to God and be willing to accept not the whole of the world's burden but that part which God has marked out for us to carry, we shall be able to accept His call to maintain our peace and do our work effectually.

It is necessary to point out that our responsibility is a relative one only, for as we think of the world-wide disintegration of the human family the prospect before us could easily fill us with alarm and despondency, if we were not sure first of the absolute sovereignty of God, who (I speak reverently) knows what He is doing in conducting this enormous experiment that we call life.

Secondly, though we often think in terms of world issues, the majority of us are not called to be world leaders or anything like it, but sensible and faithful servants of the One whose purpose it is to unite the scattered races under one Shepherd.

In St. John x. our Lord contrasts Himself as the *Good* Shepherd in whose care the sheep find food and security, with the thieves and robbers who came before Him. I have often wondered whom He had in mind, for the words as they stand, "All that came before me are thieves and robbers" (St. John x. 8), sound rather harsh. It is probable that in the contemporary situation Christ had in mind leaders of men, political, national and even religious, who really, in the long run, destroyed or stole for their own ends the souls of men. There are many "thieves and robbers" in the situation to-day who are similarly exploiting and destroying personality. We think of the soul-destroying aims and methods of Communism, of false religions which ask so much of men and in the end give them nothing. We think of the blight of materialism which by flattering a man's importance in this life deprives him of his destiny as a son of God. We think of the reckless pursuit of pleasure which meets man's love of beauty and happiness with the tawdry and the meretricious.

Within a man's own personality there is no lack of "thieves and robbers." There is his driving ambition which without the influence of Christ becomes, sooner or later, a destructive tyrant; there is his pride which insulates him from his neighbour and sows enmity between his group and another. Above all, there is his fear, rooted of course in pride and self-love, which drives out the milk of human kindness and which in its extreme forms makes him behave far worse than the animal creation. We have to face the fact that in the individual man as well as in society there have always been these disintegrating factors, the "thieves and robbers" who, though often unseen, are quietly at work. Yet wherever He is given the chance, there is the integrating factor, the Good Shepherd Himself, seeking to make men whole, seeking to integrate both human personality and the whole human family.

The problem of making men whole, of integrating them as persons and unifying them in a community, is much more difficult than some idealists might suppose. The "thieves and robbers," the disintegrating forces, have had a very long innings. They are deeply entrenched, their cumulative infection is overwhelming, and they are by no means always recognized for what they are. It is quite literally a superhuman task to plunge into the welter of centuries of disintegration and begin to make men whole.

At the risk of repetition, it must be emphasized that what we are beginning to envisage nowadays is a much larger-scale and more widespread integration than our forefathers as a general rule imagined. The salvation of an individual soul is indeed important, but we are beginning to see that the work of the Good Shepherd goes deeper and wider than we ever supposed. It is true that His plan considers the importance of the single "sheep"; under the Good Shepherd the one sheep can be saved and "go in and go out and find pasture" (St. John x. 9). But the plan is far greater than that. There are the "other sheep" (St. John x. 16) at present astray, who must also be brought into the fold. It is not only the so-called contemporary pressures which make us feel that we are "all in this together"; to those who are sensitive to the breath of the Spirit it is surely God Himself who is widening our horizons, mentally and spiritually, and making us feel and see the breath-taking compass of His integrating purpose.

Nothing less than a world-wide principle of wholeness, a world-loving and world-loved King and Shepherd, will suffice for our modern need. In the past, so long as men were broken up into more or less self-contained units, it was not altogether impossible to secure an integration which was local and to some extent superficial. The rules and customs of a tribe, for example, the unquestioned but purely parochial authority of their king, priest or leader produced such a limited "wholeness." In our own country, there sometimes existed in a village, for example, such a circum-

scribed integration. And no doubt in many countries a similar
local harmony was often achieved. But the need to-day, as is obvious to anyone with eyes to see, is for something at once more pene-
trating and more far-reaching than that limited conception. Indeed, on examination we find that the apparent wholeness of
little communities was due at least in part to fear of other communities; and the very loyalty which preserved the local cohesion
would effectually prevent co-operation with similar communities.
In our Lord's day, for example, there was a certain cohesive loyalty
about the Jews which produced in both personality and community some magnificent results. Yet it was exclusive, "for Jews
have no dealings with Samaritans" (St. John iv. 9), and they regarded the Gentiles with, at the best, a tolerant contempt. We
hardly realize the explosive quality of St. Paul's inspiration when,
under the influence of the new integrating force, he declared that
in Christ there can be "neither Jew nor Greek, there can be
neither bond nor free, there can be no male and female" (Galatians
iii. 28).

It may be a little presumptuous and it may be a little premature,
but it seems to me that in this twentieth century, with the whole
inhabited world awakening and opening up before our eyes, we
have the chance for the first time to see the vastness of God's integrating plan. The apparent insignificance of its beginning is
breath-taking. For if we strip away for a moment the romance and
decoration of the Christmas story, we stand aghast at the awe-inspiring humility of God's beginning of His task of integration.
The things which look romantic on a Christmas card or which
sound pretty by association with delightful carols were in fact
most devastatingly humble. For a pregnant woman to hunt desperately for a room when her time drew near would hardly be our
choice for God's entry into the world on human terms! And yet so
it was. That is how He came, right in at the human level: the
Word of wholeness was born into a world of misery and strife, of
suffering and sin.

It is the temptation not only of politicians and law-makers, but

of religious people as well, to think that people can be made whole
and that they can be induced to live together in harmony, by
fiats of authority. Yet when God began His work of personal rescue, there was no trump from heaven, there were no supporting
armies of angels. In the Man who was God in human form, God
focused and scaled down to meet our human need, we find One
"meek and lowly in heart," who allowed the thieves and robbers of
humanity to close in upon Him and kill Him. He had, He has, a
frightening patience; frightening, that is, to us who have so little
faith and have such a lust for quick results. But the work of making men whole was begun.

Although the coming of the integrating principle into a dark,
perplexed and infected world began, so to speak, on the ground
level, can we not begin to see that this is, without qualification,
the only way in which God, or for that matter any power whatso-
ever, could restore wholeness to mankind? Every effort to impose
wholeness by regulation from above must fail, partly because it is
for ever external to human nature itself; partly because it neither
excites the love nor provides the power to overcome human spiritual poverty. St. Paul was right when he said the law "was weak"
(Romans viii. 3). When it attempted to change human nature it
was not weak in one sense, in that it represented the eternal prin-
ciples of human conduct. But it was completely powerless in practice because of its utter incapacity to change man's nature from
within.

In Ephesians ii. St. Paul speaks with confidence, having observed the result of God's method through Christ. Into human life
and at the human level, He, so to speak, inserts His own life with
its immeasurable potentialities for converting, redeeming, reconciling and bringing into harmony. From the world's point of view,
this low-level approach was and still is a ridiculously weak and
impracticable way of tackling the deep-rooted problems of human
nature. Yet it has worked, not invariably and not without failure,
but with a result so impressive that even a hostile world cannot
disregard it. New powers, new qualities, a new spirit came to birth

and began at once to work upon even the most unpromising
material to produce whole men, and of humanity a Whole Man.
The process has continued ever since, and though our faith is
small and our experience limited we have all seen things happen
which were never possible in a pagan world. With this astonishing
apparent weakness God is at work with a kind of loving relentless-
ness to make "in himself . . . one new man, so making peace"
(Ephesians ii. 15).

There then are the two contrasting energies at work, marring
or making for wholeness in the lives of men: on the one hand the
big noisy, apparently unconquerable passions of the world, which
are the "thieves and robbers" of man's true nature; and on the
other the quiet, gentle, but immensely powerful work of the
Good Shepherd.

But there is something vital to add, in terms of man's response.
The Church began with the supernaturally inspired insight of
Peter who cried, "Thou art the Christ, the Son of the living God"
(St. Matthew xvi. 16). Up to that moment, if we may look at things
reverently from Christ's point of view, there had been swirling
tides of emotion among the people whom He met. Popular enthusiasm ran high; He was the great Healer, He was the wonderful
Teacher, He was a reincarnation of one of the prophets of old. But
all this was an unreliable floating tide of opinion. Then came
Peter's inspired remark, and at once our Lord (God walking the
earth as a human being) seized upon the solidity of real faith. "You
are Peter, the Rock-man!" He cried out, in delight, I think, "and
upon this rock I will build my church" (St. Matthew xvi. 18). To
Christ's matchless insight here was the beginning of this world-
wide fellowship of men and women of all races. Here was the tiny
beginning of the society which would transcend all barriers of
colour, class and custom, yes, and even time and space as well. For
Peter, in a moment of true faith, had seen who Christ really was.

To see and to recognize who Jesus Christ really was and is makes
the whole vast work of rescue possible. Prophets, poets, idealists,

all have their message to give, but until someone sees that God
Himself has penetrated into human life at man's own level there
can be no real beginning to the work of making men whole. Without this recognition there is no certainty, only a feeling. Without
this recognition there is no ultimate certainty, only a hopeful
idealism. Without this certainty there is no observable purpose in
all the ills and accidents, the injustices and the bitter disappointment in this transitory part of existence that we call life. But once
this recognition has come to birth, the certainty is there, the
guarantee is there, the power is there; the authority, the plan and
the purpose are all there, and the building can begin. No wonder
Christ said of Peter's outburst of faith, "upon *this* rock I will build
my church."

It is most noteworthy that this certainty runs right through the
New Testament. It is as though men were using then a faculty
which to-day is largely atrophied, the faculty of faith. They were
not so much holding on desperately despite the evidence of a
hostile world—their faith amounted to knowledge. They knew:
they knew God; they knew the purpose and plan of God; they
knew the power of God. And although from our modern point of
view their outlook was restricted, in many ways they could see
further than we, and by the inspiration of the Spirit of God they
gained more than a glimpse of the majestic sweep of God's vast
purpose. Before we can move in the matter, before we can be made
whole ourselves or take an active, telling part in the work of making men whole, we have to recapture that certainty. It is true that
we are surrounded on all sides by uncertainty, but so were they.
It is true that we are confronted by all kinds of evil, by a world at
sixes and sevens with itself, but so were they. We may be sure that
God has not changed, nor has His purpose been altered by the
centuries. I confess I can see no valid reason why we should not use
that faculty to grasp "the substance of things hoped for, the evidence of things not seen" (Hebrews xi. 1. A.V.). This is not a
modern problem, though modern pressures have almost persuaded
us that it is. It would be a great thing if God could show each

one of us that we still have that faculty of faith, puny and under-developed though it may be, and teach us how greatly He could work if we could cease from our anxieties and our preoccupations and reach out to contact the unseen but thoroughly dependable realities.

We need then first of all to recapture Christian certainty which is not a superior form of wishful thinking, but a regrasping of the purpose and plan of God by a faculty which, though long disused, is implanted in every child of God.

II

THE ACTION
AND THE AIM OF LOVE

The passage which should be studied in connexion with the following chapter is:

I JOHN iv. verses 7 to the end

II

THE ACTION
AND THE AIM OF LOVE

St. paul once said that "faith cometh by hearing and hearing by the word of God," and that is a most important statement.
For it implies that we have within us not merely the power for
holding on to a set of ideas which we believe to be good, but also
the faculty for grasping and comprehending the truth of God. To
many somewhat depressed Christians to-day there comes at times
the feeling that they are clinging to an interpretation of life
which they believe to be the truth, but which the world around
regards as merely one of many interpretations. This is an unneces-
sarily depressed attitude, for the Christian is by faith reaching
out and touching the real world. He is in contact with the "substance of things hoped for" (Hebrews xi. 1. A.V.). For the word
of God which stimulates and sustains faith is eternal truth breaking through into this temporary world, so that the certainty of the
early Christians which we may regard with a certain wistfulness
means, not that they were necessarily men of exceptional spiritual
calibre, but simply that they recognized the word of God as being
quite literally the message, plan and command of God Himself.
It was a faith more rock-like than any human certainty which
gave their lives their astonishing quality.

To-day we need to purge ourselves of any lingering thoughts
that the Christian Gospel (and the spreading of that Gospel) is

simply a good idea to be held tenaciously rather as men will hold
on to a political theory. It is infinitely more than this; we hold
in our hands "the word of life" (Philippians ii. 16). We share,
incredible as it may seem, part of the plan of God Himself; to
some extent we are even in His confidence, for we know something of His methods and the vast scope of His purpose.

In the midst then of human conflicts, tensions and sufferings,
there comes to those who believe the word of God far more than
an inkling of what God is attempting. Once we accept Jesus Christ
as the planned focusing of God in history, our faith becomes a
certainty and we know, not indeed the whole of God, but what
sort of Person God is, what kind of plan He is attempting to work
out, and what sort of people we ought to be in co-operating with
that purpose. We learn how *we* may be made whole; we learn
along which lines the world may be made whole; and to us is
given something far more than the ability to stand in this faith.
We are, as St. Paul said, "more than conquerors through him that
loved us" (Romans viii. 37), so that we win no bare victory against
the world, the flesh and the devil merely by the skin of our
teeth. God gives us the power and the love to overflow into the
world about us.

Let us remind ourselves then of the character of God, the
methods of God, and the resources of God. Our authority for
these reminders is the New Testament, which is not only an
unique collection of historical documents containing the record
of the actual physical life of God when He became man, and of
the actual demonstrable results which followed when men, by His
Spirit, lived out His way of life. The New Testament is uniquely
inspired because through these human, unselfconscious documents there comes again and again the authentic word of God—
truths breaking through like shafts of light from the real eternal
world into the darkness of this temporary one.

The beginning of our certainty, the conviction that lies behind
the task of making men and nations whole, lies in three simple

words written by St. John, namely, "God is love" (1 John iv. 8 and 16). I sometimes wish we could appreciate this, the primal fact of all existence, with fresh and unprejudiced minds, for there are several difficulties which stand in the way of our accepting this statement at its face value—which is surely what we should do.

First, in modern parlance the word "love" has become demoted and indeed debased to mean all sorts of things. A man can have a love for Beethoven's string quartets and a love for chocolates with hard centres; he can love driving an open car at high speed; but when he wants to express what he feels for the One who has touched the deepest roots of his being, and wants, as all lovers do, to declare himself, he can only use the same word! Whether it is due to paucity of language or mere carelessness, we find the same word used for a romantic but passing affection as for a lifetime's devotion and service. Yet the image of God is by no means altogether defaced in mankind, and a great many people, though they use the word carelessly or even sentimentally, have some idea of what love really means. Their deepest experiences are all strongly connected with love, and even the careless and the superficial quite frequently have a wistful admiration for genuine love.

The second difficulty is that men have been afraid to proclaim in its astonishing vulnerability the love of God. Its generosity is indeed awe-inspiring, but in putting our message before men we have no right so to qualify the love of God, so to surround it with caveats and provisos, that it ceases to be love at all in the commonly accepted meaning of the term. Jesus once declared that God is "kind toward the unthankful and evil" (St. Luke vi. 35), and even I remember preaching a sermon on this text to a horrified and even astounded congregation who simply refused to believe (so I gathered afterwards) in this astounding liberality of God. That God should be in a state of constant fury with the wicked seemed to them only right and proper, but that God should be kind towards those who were defying or disobeying His laws seemed to them a monstrous injustice. Yet I was but quoting the

Son of God Himself, and I would only comment here that the terrifying risks that God takes are part of His nature. We do not need to explain or modify His unremitting love towards mankind.

Then again we have the distressing phenomenon exhibited by some Christians of love in inverted commas! "Let love be without hypocrisy," wrote St. Paul (Romans xii. 9), and I sometimes wonder whether he had this imitation love in mind. I think I know how it comes about. Christians are commanded to love, and unless they allow their own hearts to be both humbled and purged by the vast love of God they are likely to exhibit a purely superficial attitude of love towards those who are not Christians, or even towards Christians who are not of their school of thought. They cannot really bear to be vulnerable, as love always must be; to be imposed upon, humiliated or ridiculed, as love often may be. Yet not only do they impoverish their own lives; they are at least partly responsible for the impression which many people have that Christian love is somehow not quite genuine, and that when Christians declare that God is love they mean that behind a smiling providence He hides a frowning face!

Somehow Christians must recapture on a grand scale this basic certainty that God *is* love. Unless they do, unless they feel it and know it and show it and live it, it is unlikely that the surrounding world, burdened by the apparent contradictions and all the ills and accidents of this mortal life, will ever grasp the fundamental fact of all creation.

If we were to study, without preconceived ideas, the life of Christ as recorded in the Gospels; if with fresh minds we could consider that life fairly and squarely, I am certain that we should be very surprised. So much is read back into the story, so much majesty and even solemnity is added by the matchless beauty of the Authorized Version, that I doubt whether many of us have had an unencumbered and unprejudiced view of incarnate love. Yet I believe we ought to try, even if it means a stern effort of will and the free exercise of our God-given imagination.

Let me mention three salient points among many which baffled and bothered the early disciples and which baffle and bother us—until we see that God really did enter unarmed at our own level and that He is really love, and not someone pretending to be love with a big stick within easy reach!

(1) His attitude towards "sinners." To the religious people of His day it was a scandalous thing that Jesus, unlike the prophets of old, made no denunciation of those who were called sinners; and we too may find it, if not scandalous, at least surprising. Jesus almost never called men sinners, except in the case of the entrenched self-righteous, whom we shall consider in a moment. Perhaps I make this point clearer if, speaking for myself, I say that a high-pressure evangelist, whose technique depended on arousing and fostering a sense of guilt, would find himself woefully short of ammunition if he were only allowed to use as his texts the recorded words of Christ. With the common run of ordinary sinners, Jesus appears to have used the method of simple love. The sense of guilt, it would appear, might well take care of itself; so far as we can judge He did not attempt to arouse it. Consequently, we find Matthew, loved and appreciated as a man perhaps for the first time for many years, giving up a profitable racket and following One who called him in love. We find Zaccheus, whose keen business instincts had shut him off from love and friendship, instantly melting into astonishing generosity when love touched his life. We find the hard woman of the streets, who had possibly never known anything but simulated love, breaking down completely before the One who loved her as a daughter of God. Even the woman taken in adultery was defended in her terrible exposure by the Son of God Himself, and assured that He did not condemn her.

This method of making people whole by outflowing love was and is extremely risky, but it was a risk that Jesus was prepared to take. And we may infer that God is prepared to take this the chief risk among all the other risks that He has taken in giving man free will.

Of course, even the perfect methods of perfect love did not invariably succeed. But I am drawing attention not to results —much as the modern world is hypnotized by "results"—but to the divine method. No doubt, to the early disciples as they began to realize Who it was that they were following, the method appeared foolish, dangerous and even wrong. James and John were by no means unique in wanting to call down fire from heaven (St. Luke ix. 54) upon the village that would not receive incarnate love; while, on the other hand, Peter was sharply rebuked for suggesting that some less dangerous and less uncompromising way might be found than the way of vulnerable love in an evil world (St. Matthew xvi. 23). The single clear purpose of Christ could never admit that either fire from heaven or the avoiding of suffering could ultimately heal man's evil plight. The methods of Christ, which are the methods of God, are certainly not our normal methods, and if we want to co-operate with His purpose we should do well to study His ways.

(2) The second remarkable fact that emerges from the Gospel records is the enmity of the religious. There is a chapter in Professor Thomas Jessop's book *Law and Love* with the provoking title "The Badness of Goodness"; it explains with the utmost clarity why it was not the publicans and sinners, but those whose life-long purpose was to lead good lives, who, by a strange paradox, became the deadly enemies of God in human form. It is, I think, a mistake to suppose that all the Pharisees, for example, were self-righteous humbugs whose unreality and hypocrisy Jesus mercilessly exposed. It would be truer to say that they were men ruled by principle, often with a great many conspicuous virtues; but they differed from Christ fundamentally in that the mainspring of their lives lay in observing the law and keeping their own souls unspotted from the world, while His lay in loving His Father with the whole of His being, and His fellow men with the same love that He knew was eternally at the heart of His Father. Their religion was a kind of contract, a *quid pro quo* performance, while His was the spontaneous outliving of unadulterated

love. It must often have looked to them as though He were ready to drive a coach and six through the law and the prophets. But in fact He went far above and beyond any "righteousness" that the law could produce. When directly challenged, He declared that the whole of the prophet's message and the law's morality depended upon the two most important commandments, namely, to love God with the whole of the personality, and to love one's neighbour as oneself (St. Matthew xxii. 38–40). St. Paul, seeing the same truth in a slightly different way—and not, I think, ever quite able, despite his protestations, to shake himself completely free from the Law in which he was nurtured—declared, "Love therefore is the fulfilment of the law" (Romans xiii. 10).

It would be a profound mistake to suppose that all the Pharisees disappeared soon after the death of Christ, or that they have no heirs and successors to-day. Indeed, it is true that there is much of the Pharisee in each one of us, and by that I do not mean that we are hypocrites, but simply that we would rather reduce religion to a code, both inward and outward, than take the tremendous risk of being invaded by and becoming part of vulnerable but relentless love. We do not have to look far to find Christians who have tamed and regulated something that can in fact neither be tamed nor regulated. We do not like risks; we do not like being hurt or disappointed; and there is in us all something of the spirit which would rather label and condemn and bewail than love and suffer and perhaps redeem. We smile as we read of Peter's attempt to regulate the illimitable. "If I have got to forgive," he said, "could we not regard seven times as the maximum?" (St. Matthew xviii. 21). But the same spirit is in us, and perhaps we have not yet seen how vast and humble and magnificent and generous is the love of God, nor have we realized that we are to be "perfect as He is perfect" (St. Matthew v. 48). Yet until we have some realization of this illimitable love of God, we shall never understand the conflict between "religion" and the Son of God, observed and recorded for our learning.

(3) The third surprising and rather disquieting side of God's

activity while He was on earth as incarnate love, was His refusal to use supernatural advantages or to interfere with man's free choice by the use of divine power. We know, for instance, that at one period the disciples confidently expected an earthly kingdom to be set up, and although their hopes of this became more and more deferred, yet His death came to them as a kind of "end-of-the-world" disaster, so that every loyalty was driven out by their fear and disappointment. And His appearances after the Resurrection were to men broken-hearted and utterly demoralized by the collapse of their hopes. Despite His constant reminders that His Kingdom was a spiritual kingdom, it appears that somehow they expected Him to take the power and reign. It is true that only one of the twelve experienced such a bitter reversal of his hopes that he was prepared to betray the One he loved for a paltry sum of cash, but of the others, in their hour of desolation, one denied him publicly three times, and the others "left him, and fled" (St. Matthew xxvi. 56 and 70).

I am far from judging the disciples harshly, and I would be slow to suggest that you and I would have behaved any differently in the circumstances, but I find the wholesale desertion at the end of Christ's life an almost certain indication that they could not understand this basic fact about God: He does not use force to accomplish His purpose. I hope I am not being unduly imaginative when I suggest that it must have crossed their minds many times in those last dark days that it would literally be the easiest thing in the world for God to intervene and prevent the murder of His perfect Son. What a justification of His claims, what a demonstration of the power of light over darkness, what a rousing victory for the God who had visited His people! But no celestial rescue party left the courts of heaven, no angel interfered in the final tragedy. And in the last blackness He cried, "My God, my God, why hast thou forsaken me?" (St. Matthew xxvii. 46).

It is, of course, easy for us to be wise after the event and to know that "thus it must be" (St. Matthew xxvi. 54). But I think it is still true that we are puzzled by the apparent inaction of God. From the crude cry which we heard so often during the war years, "If there is a God, why doesn't He stop Hitler?" to the unspoken questioning in many a Christian heart when a devoted servant of Christ dies from accident or disease at what seems to us a most inopportune moment, there is this universal longing for God to intervene, to show His hand, to vindicate His purpose. I do not pretend to understand the ways of God any more than the next man, but it is surely more fitting as well as more sensible for us to study what God does do and what He does not do as He works in and through the complex fabric of this disintegrated world, than to postulate what we think God ought to do and then feel demoralized and bitterly disappointed because He fails to fulfil what we expect of Him. I am certain that God who is our Father and understands us perfectly views, if I may dare to say so, with the utmost sympathy our desires to see evil dramatically punished, or at least prevented, and good triumphantly vindicated and conspicuously rewarded. But hard though it is, He has to teach us that He will no more interfere with other people's freedom than He does with our own.

I do not, however, want to leave you with a picture of a world at the mercy of the evil forces within it, and into which God never penetrates because He has promised not to interfere. The true picture is that of a world granted the immense and risky gift of free will, which is at all times surrounded by the love of God. While it is true that God forces His way into no man's personality, yet He is always ready, where the right conditions are fulfilled, to enter and redeem and transform. The chief of the right conditions is what the New Testament calls faith; the willingness to use the faculty which can touch God and which can, as it were, provide an opening through which the ever-present loving purpose can enter and operate. This love may seem to us remote and inactive, but that is because we forget the conditions under which it can operate, because we forget its incredible hu-

mility, as well as under-estimate its true power. Because we all
tend to model our ideas of God upon what we see of men, we
imagine that He who has the most power will of necessity most
obviously demonstrate that power. But if we model our idea of
the character of God upon what we see of Jesus Christ, we have a
very different picture. We see the astounding humility of God
who "stands at the door and knocks" (Revelation iii. 20), and will
not enter until He is invited. We see a character not in the least
concerned with demonstrations of the kind of power which im-
press men superficially, but fully ready to supply any number of
demonstrations of inward transformation, of arousing love and
hope and enthusiasm, and of providing adequate resources for
carrying through the inward spiritual task.

One further comment: St. John declares that "every one that
loveth is begotten of God, and knoweth God" (1 John iv. 7). And
indeed, a whole sermon could be preached on that pregnant sentence. But I use it here as a kind of tail-piece to show that this
love of God, of which we have been thinking and of which so
much can be expected, is not so different in quality that we cannot
recognize it as love when we meet it. It is love, our old familiar
friend, higher and better, more splendid and more generous, but
still love, the most precious thing that we know, the quality which
even in our duller moments we know can outlast anything. It is
not so much that we do not understand what love is, but that we
are slow to grasp love's methods of working. We are tempted by
love of power, by the show of results, by the short cut, by the pleas-
ing exterior; but love is deceived by none of these things and takes
awful patient ways, of which we know very little. Yet, though
we are blind and ignorant and stupid, it is of unspeakable comfort
and gives rise to unspeakable hope in our hearts to know, not
only that God is wonderful and beautiful and good, but that He
actually is that strange quality which lives in our inmost heart
—love itself.

III

THE WORK
OF RECONCILIATION

*Passages which should be studied
in connexion with the following
chapter are:*

2 CORINTHIANS v. verses 14 to the end,
and 2 CORINTHIANS vi. verses 1 to 10

III

THE WORK
OF RECONCILIATION

SO FAR WE HAVE SEEN THAT THE LOVE OF GOD, WHICH IS "UNRESTING, unhasting, and silent as light," is at all times pressing gently upon the complex and disintegrating scheme of human affairs; that He did, as a matter of sober fact, enter once into the stream of human history as love incarnate in a human being.

He thus began by a kind of personal insertion of Himself a process of integrating men and nations which continues with increasing spiritual momentum to this day. This coming of the light into the darkness was of course no mere "flash in the pan." For wherever men accepted this human figure as the very nature of God expressed in human terms, the same love, the same power of reconciliation and reconstruction became immediately active. Christ Himself said of the man who believes in Him that "greater works . . . shall he do; because I go unto the Father" (St. John xiv. 12). There is, I think, no need to visualize what we call the Incarnation as a sudden flash of light to be succeeded thereafter by nothing but inferior reflections. It is true that Jesus called Himself "the light of the world" (St. John viii. 12), but using the identical words He also called His followers "the light of the world" (St. Matthew v. 14). And we must not through any false modesty deny the import of His promise when speaking of His faithful follower—"the works that I do shall he do also" (St. John xiv. 12).

Part of the astonishing humility of the love of God lies, not only in His human-level approach in coming down to where we are, but in His perfect readiness to use ordinary people like ourselves as channels and instruments in our day and generation in the vast sweep of His unchanging purpose. We may think it is a proper modesty on our part to assume that all work done in His Name must always be inferior in quality and effect to His own work done upon this earth. But I believe that by such thinking we are really belittling His amazing magnanimity and even cramping the operation of His Spirit, because we have not properly grasped the generosity of His purpose. "Beloved," wrote St. John, *"now are we children of God"* (1 John iii. 2). This is the kind of truth that we take as being only figuratively true, whereas I am quite certain it is nothing less than an absolute fact, far more true indeed than any "assured result" of scientific investigation. Such a high calling must simultaneously make us swell with pride and fall on our knees in humility.

We must then consider the work of reconciliation which is the initial step towards re-integration, first as begun by the unique work of Christ culminating in the Cross, and then as the work carried through by generation after generation of those who believe in Christ, until we come to our own specific work of reconciliation in our world of to-day.

In speaking of Christ's supreme act of reconciliation, we are, of course, talking of something which can never be repeated, though we know that its never-to-be-forgotten occurrence in time is a visible historical demonstration of the eternal attitude of God. And here, at the risk of appearing to contradict myself, I have to point out that this strange work of Christ is nothing that we ourselves can re-enact. We can and should reproduce the works of Christ since the power and the motive are supplied by His unchanging love, but we are in no position and never could be in a position to build the bridge of reconciliation between the holiness of God and the sinfulness of man. We shall—as we shall see presently—share to some extent in the cost of the working out of reconciliation and redemption, just as St. Paul can say that he is filling up on his part "that which is lacking of the afflictions of Christ" (Colossians i. 24). But of the strange, awe-full mystery of the Cross we can bear no part. "God was in Christ reconciling the world unto himself" (2 Corinthians v. 19). And no one but a fool would think that he could have any part or lot in that infinitely costly work.

Although this is not the occasion to expound theories of the Atonement, it is necessary to stress the *fact* of reconciliation achieved by Christ on the Cross. The theological theories of atonement, held from the days of the early Fathers to the present day, vary enormously, and probably few of us would agree in any exact defining of something which does in fact always elude definition. But we should all agree, and this is of central importance, that at the Cross we are face to face with an action that could only be initiated and carried through by God.

I have already said that Jesus Himself very rarely called men sinners, and He certainly did not attempt deliberately to arouse a sense of guilt. Nevertheless, it is universal for a human being, as he awakens on the God-ward side, to experience a sense of guilt. Almost every religion bears testimony to this world-wide sense of human failure, and there are many pathetic and desperate attempts to close the gap that man's sin has made between himself and God. In a so-called civilized country, the primitive sense of guilt and the need for reconciliation are often overlaid or even deeply buried. But those of us who deal with the problems of human souls know that sooner or later this basic need is sure to show itself. And millions have found, as they accept the supreme sacrifice of the Cross, that the haunting sense that "something ought to be done about it" is by this act miraculously set at rest. What we feel ought to be done, but what we know we could never do, we find *has been done* through this mysterious sacrifice.

At the most the human soul can only construct a desperate bridgehead towards God, but the gulf remains unspanned. But in Christ we sense intuitively, even perhaps super-rationally, that the bridge has been well and truly built and that through Him we have access to the Father (Romans v. 2, and Ephesians ii. 18, and iii. 12). Moreover, the act takes on a personal significance as the soul awakens to God. "The Son of God, who loved me, and gave himself up for me" (Galatians ii. 20), wrote St. Paul, though he would have been the first to declare that the act of reconciliation was designed to reconcile all men to God.

When we think of Christ's positive approach, does it not seem that some Christians go about their work of reconciliation with the wrong emphasis? They are convinced—and of course they are perfectly right—that the Cross of Christ is God's answer to the sin of man. They do all they can to arouse and foster a sense of sin. Consciously or unconsciously, they try to make people feel guilty, and then they consider that it is not very difficult to point them to the demonstration and means of forgiveness. I am not at all sure that this is sound psychology or sound evangelism.

It is evident from the Gospels that the appeal of Jesus Christ was an appeal to the real man who lives in each personality, covered and defended as that real self may be by pretences and disguises, to follow Him. It is a positive and not a negative appeal, and though common sense alone tells us that He realized far more deeply than we ever could how effective a barrier was man's sin between himself and God, yet He does not seek deliberately to arouse the sense of sin. Of course men felt it; of course their unreality was challenged and exposed by His reality; of course their self-love and their disguise gradually or suddenly became apparent in the light of the simplicity of His self-giving love. But His work of reconciliation began and ended in positive and active love. He knew very well that He alone could make the reconciliation between man and God, because He alone was both perfect man and perfect God. He was prepared to allow the forces of evil to close in upon Him and kill Him; He was prepared to "taste death for every man" (Hebrews ii. 9). He who knew no sin was prepared to be "made sin on our behalf" (2 Corinthians v. 21)—an experience which wrung from Him that bitter cry from the Cross, "My God, my God, why didst thou forsake me?" (St. Matthew xxvii. 46 lit.).

Yet how little did Christ advertise or even mention, even to His closest disciples, the appalling depth to which He must plunge to win men to God. It is as though love was more important than the action of love, however fearful and far-reaching in consequence the ultimate sacrifice might be. If I may use a human illustration to reflect most imperfectly my feeling on this matter: A man who has rescued his friend from death at great personal risk, does not need, nor does he feel inclined, to bring up the matter every time they meet. Or to take a further human illustration: You and I are living to-day in freedom because during the late war other men gave their lives, their health, their sight, even their sanity for our liberty. Now whether we like it or not, whether we believe it or not, or even whether we know it or not, we are free because of them. To an infinitely greater and more permanent degree the unique sacrifice of Christ has changed the relationship between man and God. Whether a man knows it and feels it or not, the first stupendous step has been irreversibly taken and the world can never be the same again since God was in Christ reconciling the world unto Himself. Men may be slow and blind, or obstinate and rebellious, but the reconciliation is potentially true already. And because of this, Jesus Christ had no need to underline man's sin, but rather to declare to them and to live out the selfless love of God.

The Cross of Christ is indeed the focal point, patent as historical fact, of the vast sweep of God's work of reconciliation, for in this central act the man with eyes to see can observe the devastating humility of God. Not only did God in the person of Christ make what C. S. Lewis calls "that tremendous dive" and become one of ourselves, but He accepted the unspeakable disgrace, the horror and the darkness, that lie behind the Cross of Calvary. Yet I must repeat that the reconciliation of the Cross is but the outcrop in human history of a vast, invisible, unforgettable purpose—the love of God—"reconciling the world unto himself, not reckoning unto them their trespasses" (2 Corinthians v. 19). Backwards in time from this unforgettable act, as well as forwards, the steady pressure of reconciliation is for ever at work. And we who are lovers and followers of Christ are commissioned with the "word of reconciliation" (2 Corinthians v. 19). Amazing as it seems, and amazing as indeed it is, we who are reconciled to God through Christ are now the living agents, the local representatives, of the celestial task of making men both reconciled and whole. "As the Father hath sent me," said Jesus to His early followers, "even so send I you" (St. John xx. 21). He makes no distinction. The reconciling, whole-making energy and purpose of love which was in Him is to be in us as well, for "as he is, even so are we in this world" (1 John iv. 17).

It is both sensible and salutary to reflect on this high calling. So often we are bogged down by consideration of our own soul's welfare, or bedevilled by the thought of our own unworthiness, that we fail to see the greatness of our calling as sons of God and ministers of reconciliation. Fortunately for us we learn by doing, even by failing, so that we have not to wait until we have reached some fantastic height of spiritual fitness before God can use us. Provided that we have accepted His act of reconciliation, and have dropped our attempts to justify ourselves, we are embarked, however imperfectly, upon the ministry of reconciliation, upon the task of making men whole. We can truthfully say, with bated breath if you like, that we are "workers together" with God (2 Corinthians vi. 1. A.V.).

It would, of course, be the height of impertinence for any man to suggest that he could bear the smallest part in "Christ's strange work" of reconciliation. That work was unique in that it could only be accomplished by God-become-Man. Yet it is true that in carrying out the work of Christ there is an inescapable cost and pain to be borne, which is in a rather different sense the price of redemption. To follow Christ does indeed mean for every man taking up "his cross daily" (St. Luke ix. 23); and the carrying of that cross is a symbol, not merely of the denial of the selfish way of living, but of a certain humble sharing of the price that must be paid in bringing truth face to face with falsehood, healing into contact with disease, wholeness to a world rebellious and awry. We are, as God's "ambassadors," not merely commissioned to proclaim the divine appeal, "be ye reconciled to God" (2 Corinthians v. 20), but cheerfully and constantly to bear our share of the cost of that work of reconciliation. In all humility we can say that, at any rate in a limited sense, God is in every true Christian "reconciling the world unto Himself."

We follow different vocations, and the particular pain and cost of our part in the work of making men whole will naturally be different too. The teacher, especially the teacher abroad, has to cope with ignorance and possibly with the darkness and dull apathy which are the fruit of centuries. There is no need for me to point out to teachers that the cost of all true teaching is a high demand upon personality of the teacher. But the very demands that good teaching makes are the measure of its value in the purpose of God, who in this particular operation of His Spirit is bringing light into darkness and order into muddle and indiscipline.

Again, the doctor and the nurse need no underlining from me of the cost of their profession. They are always in the front line of a particular battle, and since the psychological aspect of healing is coming to be recognized more and more, so it becomes less and less possible to draw a hard and fast line between the healing of the body and the healing of the whole man. Although, I believe, arguing from the innumerable works of healing of our Lord Himself, that sickness and disease are never in themselves the will of God, yet their incidence is often a sharp and salutary reminder of our mortal frailty and of our complete dependence upon the laws of the Creator. It would be an unwarrantable exaggeration to claim that the sickness of the body invariably provides a spiritual opportunity; but it is true to say that in the healing and care of the sick and diseased there is an opportunity of mediating the wholeness of Christ in a way which is peculiarly intimate and memorable.

The work of the pastor of human souls is a vocation about which I naturally know rather more. And here, if we are as Christ was, "meek and lowly in heart" (St. Matthew xi. 29) the cost is often high. To listen patiently, to use skilfully imaginative sympathy, to advise wisely—these things all carry something of the price of redemption. Those of us who try not only to sort out human muddles but to strip away misconceptions and prejudices which prevent the soul from seeing its God, know that we have a work with its own peculiar tears and toil and sweat. The preacher and the writer may seem to have an apparently easy task. At first sight it may seem that they have only to proclaim and declare, but in fact, if their words are to enter men's hearts and bear fruit, they must be the right words shaped cunningly to pass men's defences and explode silently and effectually within their minds. This means in practice turning a face of flint towards the easy cliché, the well-worn religious cant and phraseology, dear no doubt to the faithful but utterly meaningless to those outside the fold. It means learning how people are thinking and how they are feeling; it means learning with patience, imagination and ingenuity the way to pierce apathy or blank lack of understanding. I sometimes wonder what hours of prayer and thought lie behind the apparently simple and spontaneous parables of the Gospels. It is not enough for us who are preachers or writers to give an adequate performance before the eyes and ears of our fellow writers and preachers; instead we have the formidable task of reconciling the Word of truth with the thought-forms of a people estranged from God; interpreting without changing or diluting the essential Word.

These are but a few examples from our many callings, each with its particular cost. "There are diversities of gifts, but the same Spirit" (1 Corinthians xii. 4); the measureless varieties of God's wisdom are at work in them all. Doubtless there are times when we all bewail the particular pains and distresses of our calling, and even think enviously of someone else's vocation, but the plain fact is that if we are called of God to bear a part in His purpose there can be no evasion of its cost. I do not suppose a little good-tempered "moaning" is particularly offensive to God. Indeed, Christ Himself once sighed wearily: "O faithless generation, how long shall I be with you? how long shall I bear with you?" (St. Mark ix. 19). But it is of great importance, indeed it is essential to our life as Christians, that we should recognize cheerfully and realistically that no worth-while work is accomplished without patience and sacrifice; and, more important still, that we should realize with a sudden quickening of the pulses that the cost we bear is, not a kind of occupational nuisance, but the honour of sharing God's cost in bringing men to Himself and changing them from wayward human beings into sons of Himself.

Let us then be clear as to what is involved in making our vocation serve God's purpose of reconciliation. Christianity is full of joy, but it is not a joy-ride. Christ was, I believe, full of humour, but He was inescapably "a man of sorrows" (Isaiah liii. 3). It is as if we were called to be, as Mr. Churchill said in one of the darkest hours of the late world war, both grim and gay. The grimness comes from our knowledge of the strength of the forces arrayed against us: the stubbornness of human self-will, the sheer dead weight of apathy which above all else would quench the fires of our spirit. But gay we must be too, because day by day we have the deepest satisfaction this world can afford, of knowing that we are co-operating with—and even being allowed to share the cost of—the purpose of God Himself.

Of course we often feel discouraged. We think of our high calling and are dismayed at the meagre response to our labour. We see, in a kind of indelible vision, the unfailing, reconciling purpose of God, and we are surrounded by thousands who see no such thing. For all our labours, for all our heartbreaks and our pain, we have so little to show. The remedy is to "consider him" (Hebrews xii. 3), and not to lash ourselves with useless feelings of guilt, failure and frustration. Consider Him. Was He, incarnate love in person, a success? Should we, if we did not know the answer already, consider His mission successful, when at the time of crisis "all the disciples forsook him, and fled"? (St. Matthew xxvi. 56, A.V.) Are we expecting more favourable results than He achieved? Or are we prepared, as He was, to "dare to take the awful patient ways of God" and be content to do the Father's will?

We must not be infected by the world's valuations of either speed or success. The responsibilities which faced Christ as a human being would be, if we stop to think, enough to drive the most balanced man out of his mind. But He maintained His poise, His joy and His peace. He did the Father's will; and that is both the most and the highest that we can do.

IV

INNER RESOURCES
FOR THE TASK

Passages which should be studied in connexion with the following chapter are:

1 JOHN iii. verses 1 to 10
GALATIANS iii. verses 26 to the end,
and GALATIANS iv. verses 1 to 7

IV

INNER RESOURCES
FOR THE TASK

As WE GROW UP, OUR MINDS DEVELOP IN A SCORE OF DIFFERENT ways. Our experience and our insight into people, ideas, and problems grow deeper. At the same time, unless we have allowed ourselves to become bogged down by some rigidity in our religious thinking, our ideas of God expand greatly, and there come times when we realize with an awe-struck humility that what we once worshipped as God was only, so to speak, the shimmering hem of His garment. If we are foolish we cling with desperate loyalty to the limited conception of God that we have at present, but if we are wise, we "launch out into the deep" (St. Luke v. 4, A.V.), and allow every true experience of life, every touch or sight of goodness, truth and beauty, to open fresh windows upon the illimitable magnificence of God. We cannot hold too big a conception of God, but the more our hearts and minds and imaginations are used, the more astounding becomes the central fact of our faith—that so infinite a God allowed Himself to be, so to speak, scaled down to fit the narrow limits of humanity. For all His vastness and mystery, He has made Himself known in an unforgettable character by which all men can see what sort of Person it is "with whom we have to do" (Hebrews iv. 13). It is as though, having once accepted this tremendous fact, we view all that we can see or discover of the complex wisdom of God through a Christ-shaped aperture.

This much we see as our experience unfolds, and there also expands before our minds the "one increasing purpose." What may well have come to each one of us personally as an experience of Christ is seen to be a tiny part of a vast pattern and plan of redemption embracing men of every race and colour, requiring centuries for its operation in time, and having always as its source and background the timeless life of eternity.

Beneath the vast sweep of the divine plan, we who are followers of Jesus Christ see ourselves as both humble and uplifted. We are humbled because at the very most we can only play a tiny part in the great scheme of salvation; and, as our Lord once pointed out (with a smile, I imagine), when we have done all that has been commanded we can still only reflect that "we are unprofitable servants" (St. Luke xvii. 10). At the same time we are uplifted because through the incredible generosity of God we are called in our day and generation to take part in this tremendous purpose; and, more than that, are made His sons, not figuratively but actually sons of God "and joint-heirs with Christ" (Romans viii. 17).

As we look at the world with adult eyes, by far the most important thing in life plainly becomes this grand scheme of reconciliation and redemption. And for ourselves the most important thing is to be sure that we are taking our full part—whatever the vocation to which we are called—in working together with God.

Such a high and tremendous task could easily fill us with despair if it were not for the fact that God Himself "worketh in you both to will and to work, for his good pleasure" (Philippians ii. 13). We have thought already of the immensity of God outside us, of what is known technically as the transcendence of God, but what is so often lacking in present-day Christians is an adequate sense of God within us, that is, what is known technically as the immanence of God. Unhappily, in our day the Christian religion is all too often reduced to a performance to please an external God, while to the early Christians it was plainly the invasion of their lives by a new quality of life—nothing less than the life of God Himself. I believe this lack of faith in God-within-us is largely unconscious; for while we should be the first to recognize that lack of faith on man's part inhibited even the powers of Christ Himself, yet I do not think we realize that this same lack of faith in Christ-within-us prevents the operation of His power, and our proper development as sons of God. There is far too much strenuous, even hysterical, effort, and far too little quiet confidence in the Christ within us. Certainly Christians admit that they need the help of God in the tasks to which they are called, and certainly they seek it. But I have an uneasy feeling that many do not really believe that God Himself actually operates within their personalities. It is almost as though they visualize themselves, like Christian in *The Pilgrim's Progress,* as treading a dangerous and narrow path and winning the Celestial City only by the skin of their teeth. I doubt very much whether they see themselves as sons and daughters of the Most High, not merely receiving occasional help from God, but continually and without intermission indwelt by the living Spirit of God.

In the experience of St. Paul and his followers, the revolutionary thought—"the mystery which hath been hid from all ages" (Colossians i. 26)—is that God is no longer the external power and authority, but One who lives *in* them, transforming their thinking and feeling, renewing their minds, inspiring their hearts, and effectually preventing them from being conformed to this fleeting world. Such a conviction is indeed revolutionary, and we may well ask ourselves whether this revolution in thought has taken place effectually within each one of us; for so long as we do not really believe this truth in our heart of hearts, it remains a theological idea or a beautiful thought and has no noticeable effect upon our lives.

Startling results are bound to follow in human life once the truth is accepted that God actually lives in and operates through personality. In considering some of them I am not going to be unduly bothered by theological accuracy, any more than it seems to me St. Paul was concerned with Trinitarian exactitude. He talks freely of God being in people, of Christ being in people, and of the Spirit being in people, and I think it would be most unfair to his spontaneous writings to try to read back into them any theological implications in his varied usage. God is one God; and although we have evolved the doctrine of the Blessed Trinity in order to safeguard the truths that we know about God against inadequate and false conceptions, yet I am sure that when we are considering the actual fact of God living in us, to be theologically scrupulous is beside the point. We could, after all, be quite meticulous in theological expression and yet never really accept the fact that the infinite God is alive and powerful within every Christian.

I begin then by mentioning a startling sentence from St. John's first Epistle. It is this: "Whosoever is begotten of God doeth no sin because his seed abideth in him; and he cannot sin because he is begotten of God" (1 John iii. 9). As we think into it we shall find that this is an altogether staggering sentence, meaning, I am sure, that the Christian is able not to sin because God's "seed remaineth in him"; or, if we change it into modern idiom, *because God's heredity is permanently in him.* This is one of the revealed truths of God which many Christians are inclined to take with a grain of salt, thereby robbing it of any real effectiveness. I believe it to be not only true but perfectly reasonable and logical. For if we are, through Christ, sons of God, that is to say, not sons of God by courtesy title but really sons of God, there must be in us something of the heredity of God. Plainly this heredity we derive from Him is both incapable of sin and able not to sin. And it is a factor upon which we can reckon with every confidence. It is, of course, true that there are other factors within us, of which we are only too well aware and which to my mind are often unduly stressed. Indeed, I think we do ourselves and God a disservice by continually harping upon our own sinfulness. We do very much more good if we honestly believe and reckon upon our capacity, through Christ, of sinlessness. So often one has heard Christians taking an almost morbid delight in their discoveries of their own sinfulness, yet how rarely has one heard of Christians delighting in their own God-given capacity not to sin. God's heredity is in you and me, a potent and in the last resort undefeatable factor in our personalities. Just as surely as human traits of character will "come out" in our children, so surely will the likeness of Christ be exhibited in those who are God's sons through Him.

We are slow to believe this, and we tend to play it down as though it were somehow presumptuous on our part to believe that the very nature of God is in us. We may, and we should, feel unworthy of such high honour, but the whole glory and beauty of the Gospel is that it is God's free gift. There is no question here of deserving—nobody deserves this gift of God. There is no question of being worthy, for no one is worthy of such an honour. It is all part of God's amazing generosity that in order to make His vast plan of reconciliation practicable through frail and often unreliable human agents, He not only calls them sons of God, but makes them sons of God. He does not give them a mere tantalizing title; He implants a dependable heredity within them.

The continual unremitting work of the Spirit within us—if we give Him the right conditions in which to work—is to change us into becoming quite naturally, and as a matter of course, sons of God. The attractive fruits of the Spirit which St. Paul lists in Galatians v. 22–23 are real fruits. They are indeed supernaturally produced, but they are not supernatural qualities. The love, joy, peace, which St. Paul had observed in the lives of those who were open on the God-ward side are easily recognizable as human qualities, *and yet they are the very qualities of which human nature without Christ so quickly runs short.* We almost automatically assume that these are not fruits at all but accomplishments produced by strenuous labour and stern self-denial. But in fact I am convinced that they are the outward and visible signs of the indwelling of human personalities by the living Spirit of God. I have already spoken of that horrid thing, love in inverted commas, but as long as we regard the Christian religion as a performance instead of an experience we shall tend to produce, not only love, but joy, peace, long-suffering and all the rest as artificial attitudes, or at the most hot-house fruit. This again is because we impose upon ourselves standards and restrictions instead of being inwardly free and relaxed in the liberty of the Spirit. "Consider the lilies of the field, how they grow; they toil not, neither do they spin: yet I say unto you, that even Solomon in all his glory was not arrayed like one of these" (St. Matthew vi. 28–29). The spontaneous natural flower and fruit of a life open to the Spirit of God are as much to be preferred to the tense, over-anxious performance of Christian values, as the beauty of the wild flower is superior to Solomon's imposing magnificence.

All this may seem strange and even a little fantastic to us to-day, because we are infected far more than we know by the closed-system mode of thought by which we are surrounded. The world in its wisdom has learned many things through the centuries, but particularly through the last fifty years man has come to regard all the complexity of this life as a self-contained system in which "cause and effect" can be shown to be responsible for all phenomena. We know more and more of the laws which govern the cause and effect, but less and less are we inclined to believe that there can be any penetration of this closed world by anybody or anything from outside. This way of thinking has affected us far more than we realize, and consequently we are not only much slower to believe in the power of God and in these breath-taking promises and gifts in which the New Testament specializes, but our whole personalities have grown closed and insensitive on the God-ward side.

The unpleasant price we pay for this know-all attitude is, of course, for the ordinary man of the world the blankest materialism, while for the Christian, as we have seen already, it reduces a dynamic living faith to a rather wearisome performance. We need to make a really determined effort of faith to break through this crust of modern unbelief, and to recapture that New Testament attitude of mind by which God is confidently reckoned upon to provide the necessities for the new life. We can, alas, so easily reflect wistfully that "times were different then," and thus excuse ourselves from the consequence of believing in a God alive and active to-day. It is true that times were different then, but I think we can be quite certain that, although the enemies and hindrances of the early Church were different from ours, they were certainly not less. The Christian faith took root and flourished in an atmosphere almost entirely pagan, where cruelty and sexual immorality were taken for granted, where slavery and the inferiority of women were universally accepted, while superstitions, cults and contending religions, with all kinds of bogus claims, existed on every hand.

Within this pagan mess the early Christians, by the power of God within them, lived their lives as His sons. They were pioneers of the new humanity; they showed for all the world to see the fruits of the Spirit in human life. At times the opposition was almost overwhelming, as we can glimpse from St. Paul's second letter to the Corinthians, chapter iv., verses 5 to 10, A.V.:

For we preach not ourselves, but Christ Jesus the Lord; and ourselves your servants for Jesus' sake.

For God, who commanded the light to shine out of darkness, hath shined in our hearts, to give the light of the knowledge of the glory of God in the face of Jesus Christ.

But we have this treasure in earthen vessels, that the excellency of the power may be of God, and not of us.

We are troubled on every side, yet not distressed; we are perplexed, but not in despair; persecuted, but not forsaken; cast down, but not destroyed; always bearing about in the body the dying of the Lord Jesus, that the life also of Jesus might be made manifest in our body.

Now the reason for the significant "buts" in that passage is not the personal courage of St. Paul, as he would have been the first to point out, but the Christ who lived in him, as He does in all true Christians.

To-day we face a very different world, though to analyse even briefly the particular anti-Christian elements of our surroundings is not my purpose here. But the moment that we accept seriously, and by that I do not mean solemnly, Jesus Christ as Lord, we find both within us and without us a dead and depressing weight of opposition. It is depressing because it is not as a rule violent hostility, but a soul-destroying apathy, aptly epitomized by that truly horrifying expression "I couldn't care less." And it is within us as well, because the fog of prevailing unbelief has seeped into many Christian lives and choked their joy and confidence.

Now this is where I believe we have got to do battle, and to battle first with that refusal to believe which has resulted in the atrophy of the faith-faculty, and which has become so habitual as to be part and parcel of our lives. Looking aside for a moment from the revealed Word of God, can we not see the utter absurdity of God's expecting us little impotent human beings to live as His sons, His representatives, His ambassadors, unless He guarantees and provides constantly the power so to believe and so to behave. If Christian living is to be the instrument of God's purpose of making men whole, it must provide a supernatural quality of life; there must be an invasion of ordinary human life by God Himself. If God's plan is to have the remotest chance of success, then He must provide supernaturally joy and peace and love and courage and patience, and all the other virtues which we so deeply need. I say, "He *must*," for that seems to me to be merely logical and sensible. And if we turn to the Epistles of the New Testament, which are the earliest Christian documents, we find plenty of evidence of this very thing—God pouring into ordinary lives those extra qualities which the sons of God need for their living. Some phrases leap at once to the mind:

Strengthened with all power, according to the might of his glory	(Colossians i. 11)
Filled unto all the fulness of God	(Ephesians iii. 19)
[Filled] with all joy and peace in believing	(Romans xv. 13)
Full of goodness, filled with all knowledge	(Romans xv. 14)
Able to withstand in the evil day	(Ephesians vi. 13)
Blameless and harmless, children of God	(Philippians ii. 15)

There are, of course, many more. But can we in all honesty say that such expressions accurately describe our own experience of the power of God within us? Of course, we know something of these qualities, and possibly we dream a little wistfully of how one day perhaps they might be true of us. I am quite convinced that they are meant to be true here and now for all those who in heart and mind are allied to the eternal purpose. It is laughable even to suggest that God has changed with the passing centuries or that His resources of spiritual power have somehow petered out, and yet *that is often exactly what our lives imply*.

Now when we begin to recover our faith in God alive within us, we cannot help being conscious of His purpose both within us and through us. The working out of that purpose is vast and varied, and besides the equipment already mentioned—adequate power for the job in hand to live as sons of God despite the outward circumstances, and spontaneously to produce those overflowing virtues which we call the fruits of the Spirit—we will consider two particular activities of God within us which are of very great importance.

The first is the ability to think and feel according to the mind of Christ, and to remain unaffected by the prevailing climate of opinion. In writing to the Romans, St. Paul once said: "Be not conformed to this world: but be ye transformed by the renewing of your mind" (Romans xii. 2, A.V.). Notice that he does not say, "transform yourselves," but allow yourselves to be transformed. The world inevitably tends to make people conform in their thinking and feeling to its habit and outlook, to its own pattern. The man who lacks inner resources and a vision of God will inevitably, sooner or later, conform to the contemporary pressures. We see it happening before our eyes. Modern materialism has already produced the mass-mind.

But to St. Paul at least there is an immensely potent factor working in the opposite direction, the moulding of man's character and outlook from within. This to him was nothing less than the ever present, ever fresh, ever new Spirit of God Himself, well able not merely to counteract the pressures of the surrounding world, but to renew and rearm in spite of it. Nor does St. Paul regard this inward power as a mere balancing force which enables a man to retain his spiritual balance and nothing more. No, it is an overwhelming victory: "we are more than conquerors through him that loved us" (Romans viii. 37). The power is far more than enough to keep a man in spiritual health; it spills over; it is the Spirit of love and power as well as of a sound mind (2 Timothy i. 7). We can be confident that St. Paul, whose experience of life was both deep and varied, knew what he was talking about here, and we can rely on his evidence of observed spiritual power in human life. Pressed as we are by an unbelieving and often apathetic world, we all need to see ourselves transformed by the renewing of our minds by the same Spirit. Do we believe that to be possible in this year of grace?

The second activity of the Spirit which seems to me to be pressing more and more upon the consciousness of Christians is His unifying purpose. To quote St. Paul again: "There can be neither Jew nor Greek, there can be neither bond nor free, there can be no male and female: for ye all are one man in Christ Jesus" (Galatians iii. 28). It is not within my special province to speak of the heightening of racial tensions on the one hand, or the breaking down of prejudices on the other. Such a subject needs expert treatment. Nor am I qualified to speak, except as an ordinary parish priest, of the deep and growing desire for unity in Christ which is expressing itself on all hands, while at the same time die-hards of various parties are putting up what we may hope are their last defences. But anyone with half an eye can see that there is beginning to emerge a new sense of common humanity on the one hand, and at the same time a steadily increasing pressure towards unity within the Church itself.

It would be fascinating to explore the possible inter-relation of these two phenomena of our day. While I have neither the knowledge nor the experience to do that, it is at least possible to surmise that both these movements are taking place under the gentle but insistent pressure of the same Spirit. I am a firm believer in what I may perhaps call the extra-mural work of God's Spirit, and it would not surprise me to find that in His passion for the wholeness of all His creatures God is bringing about, by any and every means that He may use under the limits that He has set Himself, the unity of mankind. There is a school of psychology which advances the attractive hypothesis that all men share a common unconscious mind, and that they are therefore linked in one beneath the level of what we call personality. This may or may not be true. But it is most certainly true of those who through Christ are the sons of God. At all times they are brothers; at all times they share the family likeness, and together they comprise the "one new man" which St. Paul had seen as it were in embryo. It is said to be a mark of maturity to recognize ever more fully our common humanity with our fellows, and that, I think, is true. Surely the Christian, the son of God, indwelt by God, transformed in heart and mind by the God who lives within Him, the pioneer of the new humanity, should be the first to realize what the Spirit is driving at—the making whole of all men in Christ.

V

Completeness in Christ:
In Time and in Eternity

Passages which should be studied in connexion with the following chapter are:

1 CORINTHIANS xii. verses 4 to 27
2 CORINTHIANS iv. verses 16 to the end,
and 2 CORINTHIANS v. verses 1 to 10

V

COMPLETENESS IN CHRIST:
IN TIME AND IN ETERNITY

IN VARYING DEGREE WE ACHIEVE A MENTAL AND SPIRITUAL VISION
of the vast scale of the operation by which God intends to estab-
lish His purpose of wholeness in this disintegrated and disrupted
world. From our present limited point of view this will always
seem not only a slow but even an inefficient process. Once we
have accepted what we believe to be factually true, and have
grasped the purpose behind the Spirit's constant movement, we
are tortured, or at least continually irritated, by the contrast between what we observe happening in the world and what we believe, and indeed can see in imagination, could and should happen
if the rule of Christ were accepted. If we are enthusiastic, we are
continually tempted to force the pace, and it is perhaps salutary
to remind ourselves that although we understand to some extent
the great increasing purpose, yet it will always remain somewhat
mysterious, inexplicable and indeed unsatisfactory to our natural
minds. This is particularly true in an age such as ours which is
hag-ridden by regulations, forms, numbers, Gallup-polls, statistics
and every other modern device which tries to rationalize and
regularize the complex factors of human life.

There is an apparent capriciousness and arbitrariness about the
working of the Spirit of God which laughs at our modern docket-

ing. The Spirit, like the wind, said Jesus, "bloweth where it listeth" (St. John iii. 8), and though we can fulfil conditions and, so to speak, set our sails to meet the wind of the Spirit, yet (to change the metaphor) we can never harness or organize the living Spirit of God. We are indeed sure of His gentle purpose, but the details of His plan lie beyond our understanding and it is at once more sensible and more fitting for us to cultivate a sensitivity to the leading of the Spirit rather than to arrange His work for Him!

This unpredictable and supra-rational movement of the Spirit is an element in God's working which makes the whole Christian enterprise on which we are engaged at once more exciting and more difficult. "There were many widows in Israel in the days of Elijah . . . and unto none of them was Elijah sent, but only to Zarephath . . . unto a woman that was a widow," said Jesus (St. Luke iv. 25–26), and He offered no comment on the seeming arbitrariness of the Spirit's working. Those who are responsible for what nowadays we call missionary strategy have always the difficult task of keeping in touch with the tides and currents of the Spirit of God as He pursues His "immemorial plan."

Now this apparently fortuitous element in the grand work of redemption, and which incidentally can be seen on a small scale in the working of any local church in which the Spirit is operating at all, is singularly exasperating to the tidy-minded. What God works in one place or in one person ought, we feel, to work in all places and in all persons. But we are not dealing with, shall we say, an electrical circuit in which the power of electricity can always be relied upon to do the same thing under the same conditions. We are not using an impersonal force, and if there is any question of using, it is He who uses us and not we Him. God is of course really moving, with what, from His point of view, if I may say so reverently, I can only describe as celestial ingenuity. But to us, who at the most only know the superficial facts of the situation, His actions may at times appear arbitrary or even capricious. I do not think we need to go "all solemn"

about this, or to over-emphasize our own ignorance and sinfulness. It is surely far better to accept with good humour the situation as it is—that His thoughts are higher than our thoughts, and
His ways higher than our ways (Isaiah lv. 8–9); and to realize
that though we are called to this tremendous task of co-operation
with Him, and are no longer servants but friends, we still need
to be most humble, teachable and flexible as we follow His
leading.

Another of our human weaknesses is to expect our own experience of God to be reproduced in identical terms in the experience
of another. Worse than this, we sometimes tend to think that if
another's experience is not the same as ours, it must be either
spurious or incomplete. Now here we must be very firm with
ourselves and use our common sense as well as our charity. People
themselves differ greatly in their capacities and gifts, and also
in their particular inward needs. One may need to be provoked
and challenged by the Spirit of God; another may need relaxation
and the release of laughter by the same Spirit. One may need
painful lessons to reduce pride and over-confidence; another may
need tender love and encouragement by the same Spirit. We
all tend to overlook the beam in our own eye to which we are
so accustomed, and to magnify the mote which is in our brother's
eye. Only God knows the relative size and importance of the
assorted beams and motes that exist between us, and much the
most sensible thing to do is to leave God to deal with each individual Christian with the infinite variety and delicacy of His
own love and wisdom. If we feel we must do something about the
spiritual life of another Christian, the most constructive thing
we can do is to keep our hands off and our tongues quiet, and to
pray.

St. Paul is very rarely amusing, but the passage in 1 Corinthians xii. about the various parts of the body is not without its
humour. The idea of the human body being one huge ear, for
example, or one vast eye, strikes me as not without humorous
possibilities. And indeed the sense of humour, which is closely

allied to the sense of proportion, is an essential part of the equipment of those who are called to work together in the service of God. The spirit which St. Paul typifies in this passage is by no means dead. For example, in his enthusiasm the evangelist often finds it difficult seriously to imagine that anyone could be called *not* to be an evangelist. The man of vision and imagination finds it difficult to see the value of those who do no more than plod on faithfully along a well-tried road. The man whose concern is personal dealing with people and leading them to understand God better finds it difficult to be patient with the theologian or the Christian philosopher whose work is in the quiet of a book-lined study. Yet the truth is that the wholeness which God is working to achieve is never complete in an individual, but through individuals living together as one body, each supplying the deficiencies of the others. I hesitate to speak of that of which I know little, but surely this is true too of differing racial characteristics. The Englishman, the African and the Indian, for example, may exhibit a certain limited wholeness in themselves and in their own church, but it is only when they learn to work together that they begin to realize a greater wholeness than they had previously imagined—the wholeness of the "one new man" in Christ.

This particular problem of wholeness may press upon the individual in different ways, according to vision, temperament and spiritual experience. What I am pleading for here is the recognition that there are three fairly well defined stages of the work of God in making men whole, though, of course, they are all very much inter-related.

The first is the stage at which a man sees himself, either instantaneously or gradually, as a personality in conflict with itself. By contact with the love of God, through which he is reconciled to His Father, he realizes his true self. By the power of God's Spirit within him, he is able to stand and grow and work as a whole man, though obviously at any given time he is far from realizing God's complete plan for him.

Then, since Christians have need not only of God but of each other, there is the stage where a man realizes his need of his fellow Christians and their need of him. Again, the process may be quick or slow, but sooner or later he realizes the truth of St. Paul's famous passage in 1 Corinthians xii, that there are "many members, yet but one body" (v. 20, A.V.). He realizes too that "there are diversities of gifts, but the same Spirit" (v. 4), and that it is only by true fellowship and co-operation with others that any kind of wholeness can come into being in the local community.

The third stage, and here the best of us are but learners, is to realize, not in theory but in practice, that in this world that God has made the various races, with their particular contributions, need one another to make the "one new man." There is no practicable way of achieving this except through the common realization of sonship through Christ. All of us who have had any experience of Christian fellowship with other races know the thrilling and heart-warming sense of unity which we thus experience; a unity which would not be possible except through a shared realization of God through Christ. Some parts of the Church are plainly far in advance of others in experiencing this enriching wholeness, but all of us have a long way to go before we see how far-reaching the plan of wholeness really is. There is a good deal of prejudice, often unconscious, to be overcome, and a good deal of blindness to be illuminated; sacrifices must be made and springs of charity unsealed, before this wholeness of mankind becomes a practical proposition. Yet there can be no doubt that it is towards this experience of wholeness that the Spirit of God is gently but remorselessly driving us all, and any step we take towards it is a step in the right direction.

These are the three stages normally experienced in comprehending the gist of the divine purpose. But there is a fourth stage, a fourth dimension, of which we have an inkling as soon as we embark upon "eternal life" in the here-and-now—the fact of what, for want of a better name, we call eternity. No follower of Christ goes on for long or far without realizing both the utter necessity as well as the grandeur of this immense back-cloth against which our brief life is set.

Our forefathers of a few generations ago, though they made many grave mistakes and had several remarkable blind spots, were for the most part conscious that they lived *sub specie aeternitatis*. They may have had crude ideas about rewards and punishments, heaven and hell, but at least they believed that this life was to be lived responsibly with an eye to future destiny. Their idea of heaven may not commend itself to us, but they certainly believed that this transitory life was but a prelude to a sharing in the bliss of life hereafter. And from that belief they derived both comfort and courage.

To-day the picture is changed indeed. In a sharp reaction from the idea that "this little life can't matter very much anyway," and that "souls are more important than bodies," a vast amount of Christian thought and action is spent upon the improvement and development of man in this temporary set-up. No harm in that, surely, you may object. Of course not; but if we swing too far we find ourselves party to a point of view which only tolerates Christianity because of its social implications; because it tends to stabilize the home, to improve health and living conditions, or to reduce the rate of juvenile delinquency. Before we know where we are we have lost the authentic, other-worldly note; we find ourselves regarding death, like any pagan, as an utter disaster; and, like any disillusioned humanist, becoming bitterly disappointed that men do not always "love the highest when they see it." The emphasis, you see, even among Christians has shifted to this world, and to a large extent we have forgotten that "we have not here an abiding city, but we seek after the city which is to come" (Hebrews xiii. 14).

In the early Church the sense of eternity being only a hand's breadth off is very strong. This was partly, of course, because its members momentarily expected the personal return of Christ, which would mean eternity breaking through into this little sin-infected world; partly because death by martyrdom was never very far from them or their friends, and this would mean not disaster but being received into the presence of Christ. And because of the overt and obvious godlessness of the surrounding world, they laid up their "treasures in heaven" (St. Matthew vi. 20), and set their minds "on the things that are above, where Christ is, seated on the right hand of God" (Colossians iii. 2). It is true that their Master had taught them to pray: "Thy kingdom come. Thy will be done, as in heaven, so on earth" (St. Matthew vi. 10), and they lived that prayer as well as prayed it. Yet they do not seem to have been unduly worried that the Kingdom might be barely established, the will done by a mere handful, before eternity, the Real Order, came breaking through in power and vindication.

Plainly, as the hope of Christ's coming faded, persecution ceased, and the Church grew rich, powerful and influential, this sense of an imminent reality in which all Christians were rooted began to lose its vividness and its urgency. Yet the sense of eternity was never altogether lost, and it is not until we come to quite modern times that we find *among Christians* an insistence on the value of God's work in this world and a rather horrifying vagueness about the real world beyond.

Christians to-day are naturally revolted by the kind of Victorian piety which could exploit the physical energies of men, women and children and then spend a small part of the proceeds in building mission-halls to save their souls! No doubt unconsciously they are reacting sharply against that kind of attitude. Yet in their passionate affirmation of the relevance of the Christian faith to the whole needs of man, spiritual, mental and physical—and heaven knows it is the only faith which is really relevant to those needs—they sometimes lose sight of the transitory nature of this present life, and the glory and magnificence of the life to come.

I should like to hear St. Paul reply to the Communist gibe:

> Work all day, live on hay,
> There is pie in the sky
> When you die.

I am certain that to St. Paul and his contemporaries the quality of the pie in the sky is such that it honestly does not matter if you do work all day and live on hay on your way towards it! "I reckon [he says] that the sufferings of this present time are not worthy to be compared with the glory which shall be revealed to us-ward" (Romans viii. 18). To him heaven was not some shadowy compensation and reward, but a solid "weight of glory" (2 Corinthians iv. 17), no doubt indefinable in earthly terms, but none the less permanent and utterly dependable. Such a faith was certainly no "opiate of the people" to these early Christians; the certainty of being sons of eternity gave them a fire and a cutting edge which the Church has rarely equalled since.

Again, lacking the background of eternity we grow, if we are not careful, too high and mighty to think of reward. We work for the good of our fellows and we despise the "profit motive." Yet Jesus Himself quite frequently spoke both of rewards and of punishments in the real world, and did not appear to despise consideration of either. And while He exposed the folly of earthly treasure-seeking, He strongly commended laying up "treasures in heaven" (St. Matthew vi. 20), and indicated the kind of conduct of which He could predict "great is your reward in heaven" (St. Matthew v. 12). St. Paul, for all his tremendous sense of that real world to which he belonged, was not so superior that he could not write "wherefore we labour, that . . . we may be accepted of him" (2 Corinthians v. 9, A.V.). Is it because we are affected far more than we know by the prevailing scepticism of our age about the world to come that we place nearly all our emphasis upon the present?

It may well be asked what this consideration of eternity has to do with our present task of "making men whole" in the Name and

power of Christ. Yet it is in fact most relevant, because without
the dimension of eternity we doom ourselves to bitter disappointment and frustration, besides leaving ourselves with an altogether
unmanageable burden of insoluble problems. Quite literally we
take too much upon ourselves when we refuse to believe in "the
ages to come" (Ephesians ii. 7). With true poetic insight Browning
wrote: "On earth the broken arcs; in heaven, a perfect round."
Unless we hold firmly to our rooting in eternity, we shall be left
with an awkward armful of broken arcs which no ingenuity can
assemble into a perfect round! The fact is that eternity is an essential part of man's existence as a son of God, and without it
there is no perfect wholeness. There is neither time nor room
enough in this cramped and limited life for anything but the be-
ginnings, decisive and pregnant though they are, of Christ's tremendous work.

There is a certain pitiable absurdity about the humanist who
loves his fellow men but has no belief in any life beyond the
grave; and this may be a salutary object-lesson to Christians who
have nothing but the vaguest belief in the reality that is to come.

Let us, the humanist says in effect, work for the good of mankind, teaching, healing, improving. We shall always be "working
for posterity," but that is a fine, unselfish thing to do and we
must not mind that. Very well then, let us assume that this fine
work is successful and that in the remote future the human beings
then living on this planet will have conquered Nature by scientific
knowledge. All tensions and maladjustments of personality will
have been removed by vastly improved psychological methods, and
men and women will be unbelievably healthy, wealthy and wise.
But what after that? This planet will eventually cease to be able
to support life or will be destroyed by collision with another
celestial body. This means that the sum total of human progress,
of every effort and aspiration and ideal, will be annihilation in the
deathly cold of inter-stellar space. *And there is nothing more to
come.* Of course, if men stop short of the final scene they may
persuade themselves that the eventual happiness of our descend-

ants a million years hence is a worthy ideal for which to live and die. But if the end of it all is *nothing, sheer non-existence,* surely no one but a fool can call that an ideal worthy of his adult allegiance.

But supposing this life is the preparatory school, the experimental stage, the probationary period, the mere prelude to real living on such a wide and magnificent scale that the imagination reels at the thought of it—then what exciting hopes invade our hearts! Indeed, we already have inklings and intuitions that these things are true. "In this tabernacle [we] do groan, being burdened," wrote St. Paul (2 Corinthians v. 4); yet why in fact should we groan or feel burdened unless it is that we are born for a higher estate, destined for "the liberty of the glory of the children of God" (Romans viii. 21)? To change the metaphor, we are like deep-sea divers moving slowly and clumsily in the dim twilight of the depths, and we have our work to do. But this is not our element, and the relief of the diver in coming back to fresh air and sunlight and the sight of familiar faces is but a poor picture of the unspeakable delight with which we shall emerge from our necessary imprisonment into the loveliness and satisfaction of our true Home. It will be tears of joy as well as of sorrow that God will wipe away from our faces in that day (Revelation vii. 17).

It is against such a solid and reliable background that we are called to live as strangers and pilgrims in this evil and imperfect world. Our certainty of that background must not, of course, lead us to look upon this life as no more than a tiresome interlude, and so to fix our minds upon the heavenly vision that we fail to see and respond to the needs all around us! But I do not seriously think there is much danger of that. It is the man who is *not* certain of God, *not* certain of the vastness of God's patience, and *not* certain of the reality of eternity, who grows cynical and loses hope. What, after all, can such a man say to the one who is born blind and deaf, to the mentally deficient, to the victim of incurable disease, to the parents of an only child killed in a tragic accident?

How right was St. Paul when he wrote, "If in this life only we have hoped in Christ, we are of all men most pitiable" (1 Corinthians xv. 19). But our hope in Christ is not confined to this life; we dare not limit His work to this little temporary stage. Behind our imperfections lies His utter perfection. We see His work of "making men whole" begun, but we never see it complete. We see His Kingdom growing in size and strength, but we never see it universally established. Do we need to be reminded that as time goes on the numerical strength of that Kingdom in the unseen world outnumbers more and more the Church on earth? His Kingdom, in truth, is not of this world.

We do not know the ultimate purpose of God; the most we can do here is to see and to know "in part" (1 Corinthians xiii. 9). But we can see the out-working in time and space of a vast plan whose roots are in eternity. It is something far greater, more far-reaching, more noble, more generous than most of our forefathers could imagine. We cannot shut our eyes to the breadth and depth of that purpose. The highest, the best and the most satisfying thing that we can do is to ask to be allowed to co-operate with God's infinite patience in making men whole.